T0114967

Words and Worlds of Wisdom
(An African Cosmology)

Compiled by

E.F. Fonkeng

Langaa Research & Publishing CIG
Mankon, Bamenda

Publisher
Langaa RPCIG
Langaa Research & Publishing Common Initiative Group
P.O. Box 902 Mankon
Bamenda
North West Region
Cameroon
Langaagrp@gmail.com
www.langaa-rpcig.net

Distributed in and outside N. America by African Books Collective
orders@africanbookscollective.com
www.africanbookscollective.com

ISBN-10: 9956-764-95-7

ISBN-13: 978-9956-764-95-2

Dedication

Pa Nke Fonkeng'sack [1905-1993]
Library and *tour de force*
Today a branch in the trilogy
Body, Spirit and Soul
That is this Baobab

Introduction

The impetus for this collection has its bearing on the elemental, yet central and intricate nature of communication in human relations. As far as words of wisdom go, the intricacies of such communication could not be more apparent, the justification being found in the range and breadth of the quotes herein embedded. As foremost Afrocentric scholar Molefi Kente Asante wonders, rhetorically, what could be any more correct for any people than to see with their own eyes? The sayings in this collection, together, present a distinct world view of a people. In so doing, this collection is in consonance with the patriotic duty to ensure a definitive departure from what has been referred to, variously, as the *traditional zones of silence*[1] and an *identity deficit disorder*.[2] It is a pillar in the edification of a culture that departs from mere hearing, seeing and consumption of other people's narratives about us to the creation of the narratives and, hence, knowledge.

No one quite sees the world like the African, and much of how that cosmos is perceived, reacted to and explained is through what we refer to as words of wisdom.

Some have dismissed words of wisdom as no more than poetic appetizers from old men that have no bearing on today's high-tech and even post-modernist environment. Yet, nothing could be further from the truth. If anything, these words have even more relevance – and wisdom – for an increasingly troubled, cacophonic, estranged and even brutish 'global village,' tightly in the grip of forces bent on maintaining a stranglehold on all thought processes and ensuring that they gear toward a predetermined and unipolar conformism.

We continue to describe words as either weak or powerful. In other words, they constitute a double-edged sword and do not, per se, amount to much. Their power comes from the manner in which they are woven and the context in which they are utilized. They are like clay in the hands of the potter, with the latter capable of molding the clay according to his preference - as a drinking gourd, a pot, or something else. Yes, they can constitute a principal agent in the beclouding of judgement and asphyxiation of thought – unless we work to ensure otherwise!

When we think of words of wisdom within the African context the focus is almost immediately, and entirely, on the foundational thoughts and wisdom of forebears which have today migrated into the public domain, and whose authors remain unknown, but for the cultural or geographical spheres (within the Cradle) from which these fountains of wisdom spring. Little attention has been given to the words of wisdom of and by individual Africans, let alone to their formal packaging into a central and unified volume - until now. This novel shift and focus might seem at variance with the African-centred prism where even knowledge – as the Duala maintain – is the product of a collective enterprise. Still, one needs to reckon with the fact that the individuals behind these sayings remain solidly grounded in the African cosmic experience. It is from it that they draw their inspiration, with geographical spaces and distances coming in to supplement - and in no way abstracting from - that common experience. The inclusion, then, of wise sayings by opinion leaders and actors from across the African diaspora is a recognition of an unbreakable commonality of experience – and destiny – of peoples of African descent.

We hasten to admit, then, the deliberate attempt to blur or minimize geography, language and similar divisions. Furthermore, we negate the idea that because these thoughts already exist online, that should render our approach unnecessary. Information might be available, but it is of little import unless it is readily accessible. Pooling these quotations from the disparate locations and spheres into one centralized place and product that is this book, therefore, satisfies this need for accessibility – as evidenced by similar (and more gargantuan) projects such as the Appiah-Gates Africana project.[3] Besides, it makes sense to diffuse knowledge in diverse formats especially considering the still unresolved accessibility challenges associated with the usage of the internet across vast sections of the 'global village.' None the least, the lessons derived from these sayings, assembled as they are in one spot, should help advance – even tangentially – the sense of unity among Africa's global communities.

This collection focuses on the trilogy of traits or compasses fundamental to the African perception of the cosmos. One is the shared experiences and aspirations for *freedom* by peoples of African descent in the age of globalization, the latter taking its roots over half a millennium ago with the forced and brutal incorporation of Africa into the Caucasian/racialist/capitalist economic-cum-socio-political system. Another is the mutually consensual cosmic philosophical outlook that gravitates around *balance,* not absolutes, as the mirror and compass to matters bearing on existence and life. Francis Nyamnjoh's notion of Africans as 'frontier beings' concerned more with 'conversations' and 'conviviality' than with 'conversions' and 'completeness' appears, then, as a reasonable backdrop – if not metaphor – to internalize as we seek to interpret these sayings. The third compass is the unflinching faith in *values.* The latter, in passing, should be considered not necessarily at variance with a civilization that places emphasis on *individual rights* - to the near-total exclusion of all else - but rather as an incitement toward the embrace of a sensible moral compass to life and living. Through it is the acknowledgement that even the sacrosanct individual could never exist apart from *community* — a philosophy famously referred to as *ubuntu*, among other appellations. In sum, *I am because you/we are.*

Therefore, a somber and objective reflection on each of these thoughts is bound to leave the reader with a deep appreciation for this middle ground, as well as the values and the insatiable quest for freedom on which these societies are anchored, and which constitute the fountain from which these authors tap from.

Some of these sayings might still be on the verge of making their grounding on the marketplace of ideas; yet, they offer such a breath of fresh air we could not pass on them! Many offer that golden opportunity for revisiting and reflecting on the long road travelled by the African, through time and space.

These sayings are of two categories. On the one hand are what might be termed the authentic words of wisdom (symbols whose decoding depends on a solid understanding of the contexts within which they are used) and on the other, the truisms. Many of the latter might elicit nothing more than laughter. That too is all right, as even humour can be said to provide a privileged foundation upon which both stress-free, non-domineering socio-human relations rest upon. [No, the African has never needed United Nations-sponsored studies to confirm the mastery and importance of that most essential form of human elixirs — non-programmed laughter!]. Furthermore, the African has always understood that, sometimes, you can catch more flies with honey than with vinegar!

Another novelty with our approach lies in the gentle and considered departure we have made from the near religious and not entirely well placed faith that ascribes *all* wisdom to old age and nothing outside of it. A few of our selections are actually by what we would normally consider youth in any context, as grey hair, in itself, confers neither an automatic nor the sole claim to wisdom. Nor, have we been constricted by some artificial measuring rod called celebrity status.

Again, these words of wisdom from the philosopher-kings here assembled should not be seen as mere words. From a purely psycho-communicative point of view, their utilitarian value lies in the fact that they provide us with much needed pauses as well as soft landing in the, oftentimes, contentious and antagonistic outcomes occasioned by otherwise too straightforward verbal blunders. When we realize how much of this brutishness can be linked back to miscommunication - fundamentally, grounded in words - the potential and role of words of wisdom as that indispensable thread in the paced coding and decoding of messages – and hence, the development, repair and fostering of harmonious social relationships - becomes obvious.

They further constitute true-to-form lessons and vital prompts toward our biggest project yet - living. It is our hope that each saying in this collection can and will help along the path of introspection and meditation as we navigate the countless daily interactions and challenges in the journey and project of living. Introspection because each saying in this collection could be seen as a coin with two sides. In practical terms, this means no saying has to be taken at face value – a call, once again, to the imperative of *balance*. Like virtue, each of them is capable of turning into vice when stretched too far! Incidentally, this fact also explains why we settled on an alphabetical as opposed to a thematic classification; no saying, no matter how overt its interpretation may tend to portray, can be boxed into a particular/single category.

Finally, a word of caution is in order: although one may be tempted to debate the veracity of some of the sayings in this collection, and justifiably so, still, the hammer of truth must come down softly in each instance. The rationale for this centres on the fact that, although considered a *sommum bonum,* in many respects, truth could and should never constitute the tree that seeks to replace or pass for the forest – not all by itself, in any case.

*****

1.   Fidel Castro, *El Lider Maximo* of the Cuban Revolution
2.   Afri-Canadian poet, Andy Clarke, *aka* Captain Sunshine
3.   Africana: The Encyclopedia of the African American Experience

Black people don't have an accurate idea of their history, which has been either suppressed or distorted – *Abdul-Jabaar, Karim* [1947-; champion basketball athlete, 1970s -90s]

Not only are a voteless people a hopeless people. A non-producing people are hopeless too - *Abernathy, Ralph* [192? - ; Civil rights leader]

A man who makes trouble for others is also making trouble for himself – *Achebe, Chinua* [1930 - 2013; novelist and essayist]

When old people speak it is not because of the sweetness of words in their mouths; it is because they see something which young people do not see – *Achebe, Chinua*

When suffering knocks at your door and you say there is no seat for him, he tells you not to worry because he has brought his own stool – *Achebe, Chinua.*

You travel to search and you come back to find yourself there – *Adichie, Chimamanda Ngozi* [1977 - ; novelist]

If we would just do it, we'll realize that we could – *Ahenkorah, Deborah* [1990-; Founder, Golden Baobab Story Writing Awards]

The choice is no longer between socialism and capitalism; it is between capitalism and barbarism – *Ake, Claude* [1939-1996; political economist and author of *Social Science as Imperialism*, commenting on the collapse of the Berlin Wall and the 'triumph of freedom']

Our problems go beyond democracy. Some of them render democracy unworkable. One of the most challenging problems is that we prefer to consume without producing. That is why we contest political power so fiercely. Political power gives us abundant coercive resources to appropriate and consume – *Ake, Claude*

A man who views the world the same at fifty as he did at twenty has wasted thirty years of his life – *Ali, Muhammad* [1942- 2016; champion boxer, nicknamed, variously, The Butterfly, the Bee, the Greatest]

A rooster crows only when it sees the light. Put him in the dark and he'll never crow. I have seen the light and I'm crowing – *Ali, Muhammad*

It's not bragging if you can back it up – *Ali, Muhammad*

Old age is just a record of one's whole life – *Ali, Muhammad*

It isn't the mountains ahead to climb that wear you out; it's the pebble in your shoe – *Ali, Muhammad*

What keeps me going is goals — *Ali, Muhammad*

Rivers, ponds, lakes and streams - they all have different names, but they all contain water — *Ali, Muhammad*

Wars of nations are fought to change maps. But wars of poverty are fought to map change — *Ali, Muhammad*

It is colourless, the soul — *Anderson, Marian* [1897-1993; African-American singer]

A bird does not sing because it has an answer, it sings because it has a song — *Angelou, Maya* [1928 -2014; Award-winning poet and novelist. Author: *I Know why the Caged Bird Sings*].

Living life is like constructing a building; if you start wrong you will end wrong — *Angelou, Maya*

Never go through life with a catcher's mitt on both hands — *Angelou, Maya*

We delight in the beauty of the butterfly, but rarely admit the changes it has gone through to achieve that beauty — *Angelou, Maya*

I have learned that I still have a lot to learn – *Angelou, Maya*

Nothing will work unless you do – *Angelou, Maya*

I can't stand not knowing where my air is coming from – *Angelou, Maya.*

You're not an African because you're born in Africa. You're an African because Africa is born in you – *Ani, Marimba* [African-American anthropologist]

To live is to choose. But to choose well, you must know who you are and what you stand for, where you want to go and why you want to get there – *Annan, Kofi* 1938 -;United Nations Secretary General, 1997-2006]

If one is going to err, one should err on the side of liberty and freedom – *Annan, Kofi*

Peace in the head, peace in the stomach – *Aristide, Jean-Betrand* [1953 -philosopher & pastor, President of Haiti, 1991 /1994-96 /2001-2004]

We must all make peace so that we can all live in peace – *Aristide, Jean-Betrand*

I have neither skill nor desire to turn the agony of a people into entertainment – *Armah, Ayi Kwei* [1939 -; Novelist]

There are some people that if they don't know, you can't tell them – *Armstrong, Louis* [1901-1977; African-American jazz musician/saxophonist]

What we play is life – *Armstrong, Louis*

What could be any more correct for any people than to see with their own eyes? – *Asante, Molefi K* . [1942 -; thinker-academic and author on the global African Experience]

As a people, our most cherished and valuable achievements are the achievements of spirit. With an Afrocentric spirit, all things can be made to happen; it is the source of genuine revolutionary commitment – *Asante, Molefi K.*

Your power is in your faith. Keep it and pass it on to other bloods – *Asante, Molefi K.*

The person who strays away from the source is unroofed and is like dust blown about by the wind – *Asante, Molefi K.*

An important key to success is self-confidence. An important key to self-confidence is preparation – *Ashe, Arthur* [1943-1993; African-American lawn tennis star]

Man is neither a hypothesis nor a mortgage – *Awazi, Mbambi Kungua* [1955-; sociologist, philosopher, theologian. Founder, Centre for Pluridisciplinary Research on African and Diasporic Cultures]

If we are related we will always meet – *Awolowo, Obafemi* [1909 -1987; Nigerian politician, 1950s – 80s]

Violence never settles anything right: apart from injuring your own soul, it injures the best cause. It lingers on long after the object of hate has disappeared from the scene to plague the lives of those who have employed it against their foes – *Awolowo, Obafemi*

In our beginnings lies our journey's end – *Awoonor, Kofi* [1935-2013; poet & author]

So much Freedom means that we swear we'll postpone dying until the morning after – *Awoonor, Kofi*

In Africa, when an old man dies, it is a library burning – *Ba, Amadou Hampate* [1901 – 1991; ethnographer]

We are more a product of our education than our progenitor – *Ba, Amadou Hampate*

A woman should marry the man who loves her, but never the one that she loves; that is the secret of lasting happiness –*Ba, Mariama* [1929-1981;Novelist]

Blessed to be black – *Bailey, Donovan* [1967-; Afri-Canadian Olympic champion sprinter]

Give light and people will find the way – *Baker, Ella* [1903-1983; African-American Civil Rights crusader]

Education is indoctrination if you're white - subjugation if you're black – *Baldwin, James* [1924-1987; African-American novelist, essayist, poet]

The power of the white world is threatened whenever a black man refuses to accept the white world's definitions– *Baldwin, James.*

Ignorance, allied with power, is the most ferocious enemy justice can have – *Baldwin, James*

A man is either free or he is not. There cannot be any apprenticeship for freedom – *Baraka, Amiri* [1934-2014; poet and Human Rights activist]

God is man idealized– *Baraka, Amiri*

Thought is more important than art. To revere art and have no understanding of the process that forces it into existence, is finally not even to understand what art is – *Baraka, Amiri*

To name something is to wait for it in the place you think it will pass –*Baraka, Amiri*

There are some people you respect and others you respect just out of respect –*Bayen, Sone F.* [African journalist]

Say not everything you think; think over everything you say –*Beauge, Max* [1950 -; Haitian-Canadian journalist]

Yams, potatoes and bananas – all white inside; give me something different to eat! - *Bebey, Francis* [1929-2001; musicologist, humorist, author]

We are the stories that we hear, the stories that we see and the stories that we consume – *Bekolo, Jean-Paul* [journalist/commentator]

You can cage the singer but never the song – *Belafonte, Harry* 1927-; singer and civil rights activist]

If it weren't for bad luck I would have no luck at all – *Bell, William* [1939-; American Blues musician]

Silence is a sounding thing, to one who listens hungrily –*Bennett, Gwendolyn B.* [1902-1981]

Image sees, Image feels, Image acts –*Bennet Jr, Lerone.* [1928 -; social historian, author of Forced into Glory]

Don't let the same dog bite you twice – *Berry, Chuck,* aka Charles Edward Anderson [1926 -2017; American musician]

Being old is not a disadvantage; it is extra time God has given you to accomplish that which he sent you this way to – *Best, Carrie* [1903-2001; Afri-Canadian Human Rights educator and activist]

Old carts can be repainted but they still keep moving in the same old ruts – *Beti, Mongo* [1932-2001; African novelist]

In seeking to please everyone one ends up being detested by all – *Beyala, Calixte* [1961 - ; African novelist]

Black man, you are on your own – *Biko, Bantu Steve* [1946-1977; Public Intellectual, Human Rights activist, Founder of *Black Consciousness* movement]

The most potent weapon of the oppressor is the mind of the oppressed – *Biko, Steve*

It is better to die for an idea that will live than to live for an idea that will die – *Biko, Steve*

Being black is not a matter of pigmentation – being black is a reflection of a mental attitude – *Biko, Steve*

Sure, there are a few good whites just as much as there are a few bad Blacks. However, what we are concerned here with is group attitudes and group politics. The exception does not make a lie or the rule - it merely substantiates it – *Biko, Steve*

If you surrender your personality, you have nothing left to give the world – *Blyden, Edward W.* [1832-1912; Father of Pan-Africanism]

If death could be bought, some would have – *Bokaka, Franklin* [1940-1972; African poet, composer, activist]

Not every death is the same – *Bokaka, Franklin*

It is better to travel unaccompanied than with bad company – *Bona, Richard* [musician]

There is a thin line between politics and theatricals –
Bond, Julian [1940-2015; Civil Rights leader]

Many are attracted to social service - the rewards are
immediate, the gratification quick. But if we have social
justice, we won't need social service – *Bond, Julian*

Violence is black children going to school for 12 years
and receiving six years' worth of education – *Bond, Julian*

The war in Iraq [2003-2010] has as much to do with
terrorism as the [U.S] administration has to do with
compassion – *Bond, Julian*

Recognize that the harder you work and the better
prepared you are, the more luck you might have – *Bradley,
Ed* [1941-2006; journalist]

I was afraid because I was ignorant – *Brawley, Tawana*
[1972-; American]

You can't find the sound if you just love sleep – *Brown,
Dennis* [1957-1999; reggae musician]

Hearts are the strongest when they beat in response to
noble ideals– *Bunche, Ralph* [1903-1971; African-American
diplomat]

If you want to get across an idea, wrap it up in person – *Bunche, Ralph*

Don't take life too seriously; you will never get out alive – *Bunny Wailer* [1947-; reggae superstar]

Music is more than just listening to it. People use the music for them protection at times – *Burning Spear* [1945-; Reggae star]

Culture is simultaneously the fruit of a people's history and a determinant of history – *Cabral, Amilcar* [1924-1973; freedom fighter, Founder of PAIGC liberation movement]

We are not going to eliminate imperialism by shouting insults at it – *Cabral, Amilcar*

If you stay home, your message stays home with you – *Carlos, John* [1945 -; Olympic athletic champion]

Successful people don't have fewer problems. They have determined that nothing will stop them from going forward – *Carson, Ben* [1951-; neurosurgeon]

A civilization that chooses to ignore its problems is a dead one – *Cesaire, Aime* [1913-2008; playwright, activist, poet. A co-founder of the *Negritude* movement, 1950s]

We have more media than ever and more technology in our lives. It's supposed to help us communicate, but it has the opposite effect of isolating us – *Chapman, Tracy* [1964-; Singer and song-writer]

We use people and love things, when we should love people and use things – *Chavis, Benjamin* [1948-; Civil Rights leader]

There's time enough but none to spare – *Chestnut, Charles Waddell* [1858 – 1932; essayist and novelist]

Impossibilities are merely things of which we have not learned, or which we do not wish to happen - *Chestnut, Charles Waddell*

Those that set in motion the forces of evil cannot always control them afterwards - *Chestnut, Charles Waddell*

If they don't give you a seat at the table, bring a folding chair - *Chisholm, Shirley* [first Afri-American to run for president of the USA, in 1972; first Afri-American congresswoman]

My God, what do we want? What does any human being want? Take away an accident of pigmentation of a thin layer of our outer skin and there is no difference between me and anyone else - *Chisholm, Shirley*

When one is over seventy, he is at the departure lounge, waiting for the boarding pass and, therefore, must have the courage and wisdom to speak out his mind on any issue– *Clark, Kiagbodo Edwin* [1932-; Nigerian Statesman &traditional ruler]

All books are merely delayed dust – *Clarke, George Elliott* [1960 -; academic]

History is a clock that people use to tell their time of day. It is a compass they use to find themselves on the map of human geography. It tells them where they are, and what they are – *Clarke, John-Henrik* [1915-1998; Pan-Africanist author, history professor]

The events which transpired five thousand years ago; Five years ago or five minutes ago, have determined what will happen five minutes from now; five years From now or five thousand years from now. All history is a current event – *Clarke, John-Henrik*

A good teacher, like a good entertainer first must hold his audience's attention, then he can teach his lesson – *Clarke, John-Henrik*

Powerful people cannot afford to educate the people that they oppress, because once you are truly educated, you will not ask for power. You will take it – *Clarke, John-Henrik*

Powerful people never educate powerless people in what they need that they can use to take the power away from powerful people; it's too much to expect – *Clarke, John-Henrik*

Religion is the organization of spirituality into something that became the hand maiden of conquerors, imposed on people by conquerors, and used as the framework to control their minds – *Clarke, John-Henrik*

Too much agreement kills a chat – *Cleaver, Eldridge* [1935-1998; activist, co-founder of Panther Party, USA]

You are either part of the solution or you are part of the problem - *Cleaver, Eldridge*

You don't have to teach people how to be human; you have to teach them how to stop being inhuman – *Cleaver, Eldridge*

All the gods are dead except the god of war – *Cleaver, Eldridge*

If you go out to Hollywood you'll find a lot of fantastic plastic people there and a lot of people in life generally. They find it so hard to be themselves that they have to be plastic – *Cliff, Jimmy* [1948-; reggae superstar]

The classroom was a jail of other people's interests – *Coates, Ta-Nehisi* [1975 - ; writer, journalist]

To yell 'black-on-black crime' is to shoot a man and then shame him for bleeding – *Coates, Ta-Nehisi*

Your story's mighty touching, but it sounds like a lie – *Cole, Nat King* [1919-1965; Singer-entertainer]

The truth always arrives too late because it walks slower than lies – *Conde, Maryse* [1937-; Afri-Caribbean novelist]

I wasn't always black... there was this freckle, and it got bigger and bigger – *Cosby, William (Bill)* [1937-; African-American educationist, author, comedian]

It isn't a matter of black is beautiful as much as it is white is not all that's beautiful – *Cosby, William (Bill).*

Every closed eye is not sleeping, and every open eye is not seeing – *Cosby, William (Bill)*

I don't know the key to success, but the key to failure is trying to please everybody – *Cosby, William (Bill)*

If you don`t have ambition, you shouldn`t be alive – *Dangote, Aliko* [1957-; businessman]

16

If not I, then who? If not us, then who? If not now, then when? – *Danquah, K.B J.* [1895-1965; political personality]

Radical simply means grasping things at the root – *Davis, angela* [1944 -; Political economist, Civil Rights activist]

I had more clothes than I had closets, more cars than garage space, but no money – *Davis Jr., Sammy* [1925-1990; singer-entertainer]

Reality is never as bad as a nightmare, as the mental tortures we inflict on ourselves – *Davis Jr., Sammy.*

You always have two choices: your commitment versus your fear – *Davis Jr., Sammy.*

Hypocrisy is like someone who has just come out of a restaurant asking a starving person to talk about the nutritional value of the potato – *Diallo, Thierno*

It is easy to love but difficult to be loved – *Din Din Ferdinand, aka Papillon* [composer-singer].

We ought to study the past not for the pleasure we find in so doing but to derive lessons from it – *Diop, Cheik*

Anta [1923-1986; Egyptologist and historical anthropologist]

Unhappiness does not come from the way things are but from the difference between how things are and how we think they should be – *Dollar, Creflo* [1962 - ; evangelist; author]

The process of change is made up of subtraction and addition – taking something off and then putting something on – *Dollar, Creflo*

A gentleman will not insult me, and no man not a gentleman can insult me – *Douglas, Frederick* [1818-1895; orator, historian, Civil Rights activist]

A man's character always takes its hue, more or less, from the form and color of things about him – *Douglas, Frederick*

I prayed for twenty years but received no answer until I prayed with my legs – *Douglas, Frederick*

Power concedes to nothing except to power – *Douglas, Frederick*

If there is no struggle, there is no progress – *Douglas, Frederick*

The white man's happiness cannot be purchased by the black man's misery – *Douglas, Frederick*

No man can put a chain about the ankle of his fellow man without at last finding the other end fastened about his own neck – *Douglas, Frederick*

One and God make a majority – *Douglas, Frederick*

You stand alone if you stand for the truth – *Dube, Lucky* [1964-2007; singer, song-writer]

Better to be alone and happy than being with someone and be unhappy all your life – *Dube, Lucky*

Believe in life! Always human beings will live and progress to greater, broader and fuller life – *DuBois, W.E.B.* [1868-1963; Pan-Africanist educator, author, activist]

Education is that whole system of human training within and without the school house walls, which molds and develops men – *DuBois, W.E.B.*

When you have mastered numbers, you will in fact no longer be reading numbers, any more than you read words when reading books. You will be reading meanings – *DuBois, W.E.B.*

If there is anybody in this land who thoroughly believes that the meek shall inherit the earth they have not often let their presence be known – *DuBois, W.E.B.*

To be a poor man is hard, but to be a poor race in a land of dollars is the very bottom of hardships – *DuBois, W.E.B.*

The cost of liberty is less than the price of repression – *DuBois, W.E.B.*

Many have suffered as much as we, but none has been tough enough to stay – *DuBois, W.E.B.*

It is good to be truthful but better to be fair – *Dumoga, John* [journalist]

You can't educate people that are not healthy. But You certainly can't keep them healthy if they're not educated – *Elders, Joycelyn* [1933-; Surgeon General of the United States of America, 1993-'94]

Art is dangerous. When it ceases to be dangerous you don't want it – *Ellington, Duke* [1899-1974; African-American premier jazz saxophonist]

A problem is your chance to do your best – *Ellington, Duke*

A man is a god in ruins – *Ellington, Duke*

To be great we need to win games we aren't supposed to win – *Erving, Julius* [1950- ; professional athlete]

I demand more of myself than anyone else could ever expect – *Erving, Julius*

Love is a flower garden that must be watered daily – *Eyango, Ndedi Pr.* [composer, singer]

I am black, not because of a curse, but because my skin has been able to capture all the cosmic effluvia. I am truly a drop of sun under the earth – *Fanon, Frantz* [1925-1961; psychologist, activist. Author: *The Wretched of the Earth* and *Black Skin, White Masks*]

Imperialism leaves behind germs of rot which we must clinically detect and remove from our land but from our minds as well – *Fanon, Frantz*

Everything can be explained to the people, on the single condition that you want them to understand – *Fanon, Frantz*

The oppressed will always believe the worst about themselves – *Fanon, Frantz*

There are too many idiots in this world. And having said it, I have the burden of proving it – *Fanon, Frantz*

Change does not mean reform; change does not mean improvement – *Fanon, Frantz*

There is a point at which methods devour themselves – *Fanon, Frantz*

Even the drunkard does not let the label divide him from the bottle; he is only looking for the contents – *Farakhan, Louis* [1933-; Preacher and Black Empowerment activist]

The same Nature that gives life and comfort is the same Nature that kills if it is out of control – *Farakhan, Louis*

What use is it to give a man the right to do something but not the means with which to do it ?– *Farakhan, Louis*

It isn't where you come from, it's where you're going that counts – *Fitzgerald, Ella* [1917-1996; premier African-American singer-entertainer, 1940-50s]

The only thing better than singing is more singing – *Fitzgerald, Ella*

When it comes to marriage, you do not meet the right person, you make the right person – *Fogu Edwin.* [1974 -; BBA, M. Eng.]

The clock turns only in one direction – *Fomunyoh, Christopher* [1956-; political scientist]

There is no right or wrong, only time – *Fonkeng E.f.* [Literary & performingartist, communications researcher/student]

Virtue too stretched turns into vice – *Fonkeng E.f*

The venom of the mamba is the treatment for its bite – *Fonkeng E.f*

Rock can become dust as dust can become rock – with circumstance – *Fonkeng E.f*

Grains of sand stuck together can surpass the force of a rock – *Fonkeng E.f*

Life is like the market to which we go with a calabash of palm oil and return with a bundle of shrimps – *Fonkeng E.f*

Life is a trinity of the unborn, the dead and the living – *Fonkeng E.f*

No matter what, fingers never miss the way to the mouth – *Fonkeng E.f*

Where do you prefer your cargo, hung on your chest or strung between your legs? – *Fonkeng E.f*

Love is like the huge African city; to it we continue to flock - and get entrapped – *Fonkeng E.f*

If you want to continue to love a woman, do not marry her – *Fonkeng E.f*

Kings cannot do without subjects; it is the only way for them to savour the strength and extent of their power – *Fonkeng, Nke Augustine* [Village 'library']

Water decided to travel alone and it missed its way; that is why it meanders – *Fonkeng, Nke Augustine*

The carrier of cow's intestines is also carrying feces – *Fonkeng, Nke Augustine*

A university that does not teach its students how to think teaches them nothing – *Fonlon, Bernard* [1924 -1986; philosopher, pamphleteer, teacher]

Many people fail not so much because of their mistakes; they fail because they are afraid to try - *Foreman, George Edward* [1949 -; champion boxer]

A people without the knowledge of its past history, origin and culture is like a tree without roots – *Garvey, Mosiah M.* [1887-1940; Emancipationist, public intellectual, author]

Chance has never yet satisfied the hope of a suffering people – *Garvey, Mosiah M.*

The only protection against injustice in man is power...physical, financial and scientific– *Garvey, Mosiah M.*

God and Nature first made us what we are, and then out of our own created genius we make ourselves what we want to be – *Garvey, Mosiah M.* Liberate the minds of men and ultimately you will liberate the bodies of men – *Garvey, Mosiah M.*

Any leadership that teaches you to depend upon another race is a leadership that will enslave you – *Garvey, Mosiah M.*

Men who are in earnest are not afraid of consequences – *Garvey, Mosiah M.*

I know no national boundary where the Negro is concerned. The whole world is my province until Africa is free — *Garvey, Mosiah M.*

If you have no confidence in self, you are twice defeated in the race of life — *Garvey, Mosiah M.*

Progress is the attraction that moves humanity — *Garvey, Marcus Mosiah*

There is no force like success, and that is why the individual makes all effort to surround himself throughout life with the evidence of it; as of the individual, so should it be of the nation — *Garvey, Mosiah M.*

I have no desire to take all black people back to Africa; there are blacks who are no good here and will likewise be no good there — *Garvey, Mosiah M.*

The whole world is run on bluff — *Garvey, Mosiah M.*

We must never make day night — *Garvey, Mosiah M.*

Look for me in the whirlwind or the storm — *Garvey, Mosiah M.*

I regard the Klan, the Anglo-Saxon clubs and White American societies, as far as the Negro is concerned, as better friends of the race than all other groups of hypocritical whites put together – *Garvey, Mosiah M.*

Truth buried will rise again– *Garvey, Mosiah M*

Censorship is to art as lynching is to justice – *Gates, Henry L.* [1950-; African-American professor, author; co-editor of *Encyclopedia of Africa*]

Always, if you win mentally, you can win physically as well – *Gebrselassie, Haile* [1973-; Olympian marathoner]

You must do as your people do. If my people are poor, I must be poor. People ask me, 'Why don't you find a personal coach or a private car?' I can't. Then I won't be part of my people – *Gebrselassie, Haile*

One of the main purveyors of violence in this world has been this (USA) country – *Glover, Danny* [1946-; American actor, Civil Rights activist]

Hell hath no fury like a liberal scorned – *Gregory, Dick* [1932-; American humorist, Civil rights activist]

I am really enjoying the new Martin Luther King Jr stamp - just think about all those white bigots, licking the backside of a black man – *Gregory, Dick*

I never believed in Santa Claus because I knew no white dude would come into my neighborhood after dark – *Gregory, Dick*

I never learned hate at home, or shame. I had to go to school for that – *Gregory, Dick*

I wouldn't mind paying taxes - if I knew they were going to a friendly country – *Gregory, Dick*

In America, with all of its evils and faults, you can still reach through the forest and see the sun. But we don't know yet whether that sun is rising or setting for our country – *Gregory, Dick*

Just being a Negro doesn't qualify you to understand the race situation any more than being sick makes you an expert on medicine – *Gregory, Dick*

Political promises are much like marriage vows. They are made at the beginning of the relationship between candidate and voter, but are quickly forgotten – *Gregory, Dick*

Riches do not delight us so much with their possession, as torment us with their loss – *Gregory, Dick*

A 'yes' is of no significance if the man who utters it has the capacity to say 'no.' – *Gueye, Lamine* [1891-1968; African political personality, 1960s]

Anytime you see a turtle up on top of a fence post, you know he had some help – *Haley, Alex* [1921-1992; African-AmericanauthorofRoots, *Queen, The Autobiography of Malcom X* and other works]

Either you deal with what is the reality, or you can be sure that the reality is going to deal with you – *Haley, Alex*

When you clench your fist, no one can put anything in your hand, nor can your hand pick up anything – *Haley, Alex*

Let me just say: Peace to you, if you're willing to fight for it – *Hampton,Fred*[1948-1969;Emancipationist activist]

If you want peace then you must struggle for social justice – *Hani, Chris* [1942-1993; South African political activist]

The road to success is always under construction – *Harvey, Steve* [1957-; American comedian]

Beware the clever man that makes the wrong look right – *Hill, Lawrence* [1957 -; novelist; memoirist]

There is no success without sacrifice; no wealth without work — *Holness, Andrew* [1972 -; Jamaican politician]

A good history covers not only what was done, but the thought that went into the action. You can read the history of a country through its actions — *Hooks, Benjamin L.* [1925-2010; lawyer, Civil Rights advocate]

Dialogue is the weapon of the brave — *Houphouët-Boigny, Felix* [1905 – 1993; statesman]

Freedom will never thrive in the midst of misery — *Houphouët-Boigny, Felix*

Love makes your soul crawl out of its hiding place — *Hurston, Zora N* [1891-1960; American anthropologist, author]

If you are silent about your pain they will kill you and say you enjoyed it — *Hurston, Zora N*

Some people could look at a mud puddle and see an ocean with ships — *Hurston, Zora N*

The present was an egg laid by the past that had the future inside its shell — *Hurston, Zora N*

I did not just fall in love; I made a parachute jump – *Hurston, Zora N*

All my skinfolk ain't kinfolk – *Hurston, Zora N*

Until we honor those who gave their lives in pursuit of freedom, their bones, like daggers, will continue to stab our memories – *Ikolo, Timothy* [novelist]

People say that slaves were taken from Africa. This is not true. People were taken from Africa, among them healers and priests, and were made into slaves – *Ibrahim, Abdullah* [1934 - ; composer, pianist]

They took away time, and they gave us the clock – *Ibrahim, Abdullah*

Both tears and sweat are salty, but they render a different result. Tears will get you sympathy; sweat will get you change – *Jackson, Jesse* [1941-; Pastor, Civil Rights leader/activist]

In politics, an organized minority is a political majority – *Jackson, Jesse*

It is time for us to turn to each other, not on each other – *Jackson, Jesse*

I am not a perfect servant. I am a public servant doing my best against the odds. As I develop and serve, be patient. God is not finished with me yet – *Jackson, Jesse*

I cast my bread on the waters long ago. Now it's time for you to send it back to me - toasted and buttered on both sides – *Jackson, Jesse*

Keep hope alive – *Jackson, Jesse*

Leadership cannot just go along to get along. Leadership must meet the moral challenge of the day – *Jackson, Jesse*

Never look down on anybody unless you're helping him up – *Jackson, Jesse*

Time is neutral and does not change things – *Jackson, Jesse*

Today's students can put dope in their veins or hope in their brains – *Jackson, Jesse*

We've removed the ceiling above our dreams. There are no more impossible dreams – *Jackson, Jesse*

When the doors of opportunity swing open, we must make sure that we are not too drunk or too indifferent to walk through – *Jackson, Jesse*

When we're unemployed, we're called lazy; when the whites are unemployed it's called a depression – *Jackson, Jesse*

If my mind can conceive it, and my heart can believe it, I know I can achieve it – *Jackson, Jesse*

In many ways, history is marked as 'before' and 'after.' Rosa Parks sat down in order that we all might stand up – *Jackson, Jesse*

I hear that melting-pot stuff a lot, and all I can say is thatwehaven'tmelted–*Jackson, Jesse*

If there are occasions when my grape turned into a raisin and my joy bell lost its resonance, please forgive me. Charge it to my head and not to my heart – *Jackson, Jesse*

I know they are all environmentalists. I heard a lot of my speeches recycled –– *Jackson, Jesse*

Don't talk skin to me – *Jackson, Mahalia* [1911-1972; singer]

Just because it's in print doesn't mean it's the gospel – *Jackson. Michael* [1958-2009; singer, songwriter, dancer]

If you have achieved any level of success, then pour it into someone else. Success is not success without a successor–*Jakes,T.D.*[1957-;African-American evangelist, philanthropist, filmmaker, author]

If you are not their slaves, you are rebels – *James, CLR.* [1901- 1989; author-scholar]

All the world has been converted and Washington is the new mecca – *James, CLR*

Whoever controls the images, controls your self-esteem, self-respect and self-development. Whoever controls the history, controls the vision – *Jeffries, Leonard* [1937-; Pan-Africanist historian, author]

Truth crushed to earth will rise again stronger than ever – *Jeffries, Leonard*

All business is personal. Make your friends before you need them. – *Johnson, Robert Louis* [1946-; businessman]

You don't build a bond without being present – *Jones, James Earl* [1931-; actor]

You have to know that your real home is within – *Jones, Quincy* [1933-; musicologist]

It's amazing how much trouble you can get in when you don't have anything else to do – *Jones, Quincy*

I've always thought that a big laugh is a really loud noise from the soul – *Jones, Quincy*

If the road to social transformation can be paved only by saints who never make mistakes, the road will never be built – *Jones, Van* [1968 -; Social commentator, author]

It's in that convergence of spiritual people becoming active and active people becoming spiritual that the hope of humanity now rests – *Jones, Van*

All humans have fear, and those of us who are fortunate have faith – *Jones, Van*

In a democracy you won't always get to have your way. But you should always get to have your say – *Jones, Van*

When it gets harder to love, love harder – *Jones, Van*

I've never lost a game, I just ran out of time – *Jordan, Michael* [1963-; basketball superstar]

I have failed over and over again in my life. And that is why I succeed – *Jordan, Michael*

Terrorism is not new to black people – *Jordan, Vernon* [1935-; American politician, activist]

Anything you would like for somebody to do to you, do to him first – *Joseph, Marcel* [Afri-Canadian actor & media personality]

It is not enough to be free of the whips, principalities and powers – *Kamu, Brathwaite* [1930-; Caribbean literary activist]

The other thing they try to do is make us responsible for our own enslavement. And here they collapse three kinds of people: perpetrators, collaborators and victims – *Karenga, Maulana* [1941-; Author, professor. Founder of the *Kwanzaa* movement]

They had the capacity to destroy and didn't have the moral restraint not to – *Karenga, Maulana*

Ambition never comes to an end – *Kaunda, K. K.* [1924-; freedom fighter; African political leader]

The power which establishes a state is violence; the power which maintains it is violence; the power which eventually overthrows it is violence – *Kaunda, K. K.*

Our children may learn about the heroes of the past. Our task is to make ourselves the architects of the future – *Kenyatta, J.* [1891-1978; politician, freedom fighter]

When the Missionaries arrived, the Africans had the land and the Missionaries had the Bible. They taught how to pray with our eyes closed. When we opened them, they had the land and we had the Bible – *Kenyatta, J.*

We want our cattle to get fat on our land; we do not want the fat removed to feed others – *Kenyatta, J.*

It is better to look ahead and prepare, than to look back and regret – *Kersey, Jackie Joyner* [1962 -; champion athlete]

The beautiful thing about learning is nobody can take it away from you – *King, B.B.* [1925-2015; world renowned American blues musician]

Returning violence for violence multiplies violence – *King, M.L Jr.* [1929 -1968; philosopher, preacher, author, Civil Rights leader]

Everyman must decide whether he will walk in the light of creative altruism or in the darkness of destructive selfishness – *King, M.L Jr.*

Injustice anywhere is a threat to justice everywhere – *King, M.L Jr.*

To accept passively a unjust system is to cooperate with that system; thereby the oppressed become as evil as the oppressor – *King, M.L. Jr*

Cowardice asks the question: is it safe? Expediency asks the question: is it political? Vanity asks the question: is it popular? But Conscience asks the question: is it right? – *King, M.L. Jr.*

And there comes a time when one must take a position that is neither safe, nor political, nor popular – but one must take it simply because it is right –*King, M.L. Jr.*

Darkness cannot drive out darkness; only light can do that. Hate cannot drive out hate; only love can do that. Hate multiplies hate, violence multiplies violence, and toughness multiplies toughness in a descending spiral of destruction – *King, M.L. Jr.*

Life is not something we find but something we create – *King, M.L. Jr.*

As long as the mind is enslaved the body can never be free – *King, M.L. Jr.*

Psychological freedom is the most powerful weapon against the long night of physical slavery – *King, M.L. Jr.*

Even if I knew that tomorrow the world would go to pieces I would still plant my apple tree – *King, M.L. Jr.*

A man dies when he refuses to stand up for that which is right – *King, M.L. Jr.*

Hate is too great a burden to bear. It injures the hater more than it injures the hated – *King, Coretta Scott* [1927-2006; American Civil rights mentor]

Women, if the soul of the nation is to be saved, you must become its soul – *King, Coretta Scott.*

Marriage is not a meal prepared – *Kisseadoo Samuel* [writer]

If the creator wanted us to talk more and listen less he would have given us two mouths and one ear – *Kisseadoo Samuel*

I am a farmer by birth, a doctor by training and a politician by circumstance – *Kisseka, Samson* [1912- 1999; African politician; physician]

We are dead when we sleep – *Ki-Zerbo, Joseph* [1922-2006; historian]

There is no action which does not come to an end at some point. There is no eternal night, nor day – *Kourouma, Ahmadu* [1927-2003; novelist]

No amount of insult or will stop the sun from setting in the evening -*Kourouma, Ahmadu*

Water has no enemy – *Kuti, Fela'anikulapo* [1938-1997; musician, Human Rights activist]

Freedom has a price and those who are not ready to pay it are destined for servitude – *Lado, Ludovic* [1968-; Jesuit priest]

Time goes faster when man tries to stop it – *Laferierre, Dany* [1953-; Literary author]

Death is a travel agency that specializes in the issue of one-way tickets – *Lottin, Eboa* [1942-1997; poet, musician]

We must set ourselves to search ceaselessly for truth in all its forms. Truth is the only means by which we can contribute to our spiritual and intellectual development – *Lumumba, Patrice* [1925-1961; Kongolese politician]

Unity and victory are synonymous – *Machel, Samora* [1933-1986; freedom fighter, politician]

To forgive is easy. To forget is stupid – *Maduabum, Peter* [lawyer]

It is much easier to believe than to think; people seldom think about that which we are taught to believe – *Madubuti, Haki* [1942-; public intellectual. Co-founder, Third World Press]

We fry potatoes in Dar es Salaam and still call them *French* fries! – *Magufuli, Pombe John* [1959-; Tanzanian politician]

Age is getting to know all the ways the world turns, so that if you cannot turn the world the way you want, you can at least get off the way so you won't get run over – *Makeba, M.* [1932-2008; singer-entertainer, Rights activist]

Africa has her mysteries, and even a wise man cannot understand them. But a wise man respects them – *Makeba, M.*

A man who stands for nothing will fall for anything – *Malcom X* [1925-1965; preacher, author. Emancipationist]

Stumbling is not falling – *Malcom X*

Power in defense of freedom is greater than power in *(sic)* behalf of tyranny and oppression – *Malcom X*

If you have no critics you will likely have no success – *Malcom X*

The economic philosophy of black nationalism only means that our people need to be re-educated into the importance of controlling the economy of the community in which we live, which means that we won't have to constantly be involved in picketing and boycotting other people in other communities in order to get jobs – *Malcom X*

The most dangerous man is one who has nothing to lose – *Malcom X*

If we are scared to die, we shall not rise – *Malema, Julius* [1981 – ; South African politician-activist]

The brave man is not he who does not feel afraid, but he who conquers that fear – *Mandela, N* [1918 – 2013; freedom fighter, humanist]

Forgiveness liberates the soul – *Mandela, N*

Poverty is not an accident. Like slavery and apartheid, it is man-made and can be removed by the actions of human beings – *Mandela, N*

It always seems impossible until it is done – *Mandela, N.*

It is better to lead from behind – *Mandela, N*

There is no passion to be found in playing small – in settling for a life that is less than the one you are capable of living – *Mandela, N.*

What counts in life is not the mere fact that we have lived. It is what difference we have made to the lives of others that will determine the significance of the life we lead – *Mandela, N*

A good head and a good heart are always a formidable combination – *Mandela, N*

If you talk to a man in a language he understands, that goes to his head. If you talk to him in his language, that goes to his heart – *Mandela, N.*

The oppressor and the oppressed each lose a bit of their humanity – *Mandela, N.*

To understand today's politics one must always begin with yesterday's economics – *Manley, Michael* [1924-1997; Caribbean political leader]

If today were half as good as tomorrow is supposed to be, it would probably be twice as good as yesterday was – *Manley, Norman W.* [1893-1969; Caribbean political leader]

My reason nourishes my faith and my faith my reason – *Manley, Norman W.*

Some people feel the rain; others just get wet – *Marley, Robert Nesta* [1945-1981; reggae superstar]

Live for yourself and you will live in vain; live for others, and you will live again – *Marley, Robert Nesta*

The people who are trying to make this world worse are not taking the day off. Why should I? – *Marley, Robert Nesta*

My fear is my only courage – *Marley, Robert Nesta*

Free speech carries with it some freedom to listen – *Marley, Robert Nesta*

In the abundance of water, the fool is thirsty – *Marley, Robert Nesta*

I have a lifetime appointment and I intend to serve it. I expect to die at 110, shot by a jealous husband – *Marshall, Thurgood* [1908-1993; jurist, motivational speaker]

None of us got where we are solely by pulling ourselves up by our bootstraps. We got here because somebody bent down and helped us pick up our boots – *Marshall, Thurgood*

What is the quality of your intent? – *Marshall, Thurgood*

Sometimes history takes things into its own hands – *Marshall, Thurgood*

Doing something with what you have puts you on the path to getting what you do not have – *Mawa, Bebia P.* [1972 -; TV host & producer]

Do not wait to achieve your dreams before you are happy. For it is when you are happy with life that you can achieve your dreams – *Mawa, Bebia P.*

The value of a true champion is not just in the battles he wins but also in the ones he chooses to ignore – *Mawa, Bebia P.*

Success is not doing one big thing, but doing a number of little things excellently – *Mawa, Bebia P.*

Life is like a buffet. What you choose to add on your plate is what you will eat. Not everything on the table is for everybody – *Mawa, Bebia P*

Humility is the mother of humanity – *Manyombe, Ndumbe* [1966 -; financial analyst]

What people don't know about oppression is that the oppressor works much harder – *Masekela, Ramopolo H.* [1939 - ; musician]

A people denied history is a people deprived of dignity – *Mazrui, Ali*[1933–2014; afro-centric researcher, teacher].

I am because we are and, since we are, therefore I am – *Mbiti, John* [1931 –; theologian, philosopher].

If a man is not faithful to his own individuality, he cannot be loyal to anything – *McKay, Claude* [1889 – 1948; writer]

Those who oppressed us described us as the Dark Continent! – *Mbeki, Thabo*[1942-; South African freedom fighter & politician]

'I love you' takes three seconds to utter, three hours to explain, and a lifetime to prove – *Mbuyulu, Fabrice* [1987- ; singer, songwriter]

Democracy is the dictatorship of laws - *Moise, Jovenel* [1968- ; Haitian politician]

A genius is the one most like himself - *Monk, Thelonius* [1917 -1982; jazz musician]

All water has a perfect memory and is forever trying to get back to where it was – *Morrison, T.* [1931-; American novelist]

Freeing yourself is one thing; claiming ownership of that freed self is another – *Morrison, T.*

Love of self comes first. The one who loves everybody is the one who does not love anyone – *Muhammad, Elijah* [1897-1975; Founder, Nation of Islam]

Peace if possible, War if necessary - *Muhammad, Khallid A.*

Justice is not negotiable – *Mukweje, Denis* [1955 -; gynecologist; women's health activist]

The advice I would give to anyone is to not take anyone's advice – *Murphy Eddie* [1961-; actor, movie producer]

You have to have a filter on what you let in - *Murphy Eddie*

We cannot conduct the business of saving souls as if saving lives did not matter – *Ndongmo, Albert* [1926-1992; philosopher, Catholic Priest]

We are all we have – *Nettleford, Rex* [1933-2010; public intellectual, performing artist]

If we don't hang together we will surely hang separately – *Nettleford, Rex*

We are good at sprinting but not so good at long-distance running – *Nettleford, Rex*

Everybody plays the fool sometimes – *Neville, Aaron* [1941-; Neville Brothers, American soul/rock band]

Any unarmed people are slaves, or are subject to slavery at any given moment – *Newton, Huey* [1942-1989; human rights activist. Co-founder, Black Panther Party]

Sometimes if you want to get rid of the gun, you have to pick the gun up — *Newton, Huey*

I do not expect the white media to create positive black male images — *Newton, Huey*

You can jail a Revolutionary, but you can't jail the Revolution — *Newton, Huey*

The earth we step on every day with impunity becomes our master in the end — *Ngako, Nestor* [1959; student of Life]

Language is the most important vehicle through which power fascinates and holds the soul prisoner — *Ngugi wa Thiong'o* [1938- ; Africanist writer, author]

There are some people, be they black or white, who don't want others to rise above them. They want to be the source of all knowledge and share it piecemeal to others less endowed. ... A rich man does not want others to get rich because he wants to be the only man with wealth — *Ngugi wa Thiong'o*

Our lives are a battlefield on which is fought a continuous war between the forces that are pledged to confirm our humanity and those determined to dismantle it; those who strive to build a protective wall around it, and those who wish to pull it down; those who seek to mould it and those committed to breaking it up; those who aim to open our eyes, to make us see the light and look to tomorrow, and those who wish to lull us into closing our eyes – *Ngugi wa Thiong'o*

A white man is a white man. But a black man trying to be white man is bad and rash – *Ngugi wa Thiong'o*

Time and bad conditions do not favour beauty – *Ngugi wa Thiong'o*

You cannot beat a child and tell it how to cry – *Ngwane, George* [1960 -; public intellectual]

The forces that unite us are intrinsic and greater than the superimposed influences that keep us apart – *Nkrumah, Kwame* [1909–1972; Pan-African activist-leader, philosopher, author]

Freedom is not something that one people can bestow on another as a gift. They claim it as their own and none can keep it from them – *Nkrumah, K.*

Revolutions are brought about by men, by men who think as men of action and act as men of thought – *Nkrumah, K.*

The best way of learning to be an independent sovereign state is to be an independent sovereign state – *Nkrumah, K.*

Thought without practice is empty, action without thought is blind – *Nkrumah, K.*

There cannot be democracy in an unstable environment. Neither can there be development in an undemocratic environment where citizens are deprived of taking initiatives – *Nujoma, Sam.* [1929 -; Freedom fighter]

The foundation of all good solutions to problems is discussion and debate – *Nujoma, Sam*

Peace is today perhaps the most expensive commodity in the world in general – *Nujoma, Sam*

Not all that counts can be counted, Not all that can be counted counts – *Nyamnjoh, B. Francis.* [1961-; anthropologist, professor, author]

Small nations are like indecently dressed women; they tempt the evil-minded–*Nyerere, J.K.*[1922-1999; statesman, politician, author]

African nationalism is meaningless, dangerous, anarchronistic, if it is not, at the same time, pan-Africanism – *Nyerere, J.K.*

Just because we have the best hammer does not mean every problem is a nail – *Obama, Barack H.* [1961-; President of the U.S.A, 2008-2016]

Don't just buy a new video game, make one. Don't just download the latest app, help design it. Don't just play on your phone, program it - *Obama, Barack H.*

It is difficult to be happily married; you are either happy or married – *Ogunmekan, Ade* [1974-; Systems Analyst and Software Engineer]

And up till tomorrow, whenever I'm given the opportunity to choose, I'll reject slavery – *Ojukwu, Odemegwu* [1933-2011; soldier-politician, activist]

It is better we move slightly apart and survive than move together and perish in our collision – *Ojukwu, Odemegwu*

War does not solve; it covers, but the problem remains – *Ojukwu, Odemegwu*

A real friend is not one who sheds tears over his friend's troubles but one who ensures that his friend does not shed tears in spite of his troubles – *Olomide, Koffi* [1956-; singer-composer]

If everyone knew what everyone else said to anyone about everyone else no one would speak to nor about anyone – *Olomide, Koffi*

I was born a slave, but nature gave me a soul of a free man – *L'Ouverture, Toussaint* [1743-1803; Emancipationist]

The magician and the politician have much in common: they both have to draw our attention away from what they are really doing – *Okri, Ben* [1959-; novelist]

The worst realities of our age are manufactured realities. It is therefore our task, as creative participants in the universe, to re-dream our world – *Okri, Ben*

The fact of possessing imagination means that everything can be re- dreamed – *Okri, Ben.*

Our future is greater than our past – *Okri, Ben.*

Love is sacrifice – *Oyelowo, David* [1976-; actor, screenwriter]

People always say I didn't give up my seat because I was tired, but that isn't true. No, the only tired I was, was of giving in – *Parks, Rosa* [1913-2005; Civil Rights activist & mentor]

Knowing what must be done does away with fear – *Parks, Rosa*

In truth there are no sides. No black or white. Democrat or Republican. Liberal or Conservative. Democracy or Dictatorship. Capitalism or Communism. Truth is not about you or me being right. Truth is neutral - *Peterkin, Raymond* [1952-; Caribbean-Canadian activist]

If you have no aspirations of your own, then you are bound by the aspirations of others, whether negative or positive - *Peterkin, Raymond*

Do your own thinking! - *Peterkin, Raymond*

Freedom is never given; it is won – *Philip, Randolph A.* [1889-1979; labour leader/activist]

Salvation for a race, nation or class must come from within – *Philip, Randolph A.*

You cannot walk on both sides of the road at the same time – *Pini, Jason* [1948-2013; journalist]

My autobiography was simply the story of my life –
Poitier, Sidney [1927-; screen actor]

We all suffer from the preoccupation that there exists
perfection – *Poitier, Sidney*

So much of life is determined by randomness – *Poitier,
Sidney*

I learned to hear silence – *Poitier, Sidney*

There is no future for a people who deny their past –
Powell, Adam Clayton [1908 –1972; US Congressman]

There are no secrets to success. It is the result of
preparation, hard work and learning from failure – *Powell,
Colin L.* [1937-; American soldier & politician]

A deception that elevates us is dearer than a host of
low truths – *Pushkin, Alexander* [1799-1837; Afro-Russian
philosopher-novelist]

I'm in the kitchen and I'm not walking out! – *Rangel,
Charles* [1930-; African-American politician]

We learn about one another's cultures the same way
we learn about sex: in the streets – *Reid, Ishmael* [1938-;
African-American literary author & critic]

Being in blackman today is like being a spectator at your own trial – *Reid, Ishmael*

The grass may look greener on the other side, but it's just as hard to cut – *Richard, Wayne Peniman aka Little Richard* [1932-; American entertainer]

I don't think a woman has to act like a man to show that she has strength, or that you have to be effeminate to be sensitive – *Richard, Wayne Peniman aka Little Richard*

I am not concerned with your liking or disliking me; all I ask is that you respect me as a human being – *Robinson, Jackie* [1919 - 1972; American sports champion]

We have more information but less knowledge. More communication but less community. More goods but less goodwill. More of virtually everything save that which the human spirit requires. So distracted have we become satisfying this new need or that material appetite, we hardly noticed the departure of happiness – *Robinson, Randall* [1941-; African-American philanthropist, Founder of *TransAfrica*, 1977. Author of *Quitting America* (on his self-exile from the U.S) and *The Debt* (a case for slavery reparations)

They like you to have an election, but they like you to elect the people they want you to elect – *Robinson, Randall*

You can only offend me if you mean something to me — *Rock, Chris*. [1965-; American humorist]

By what standard of morality can the violence used by a slave to break his chains be considered the same as the violence of a slave master? — *Rodney, Walter A*. [1942-1980; historian, political economist, activist]

It is often easier to become outraged by injustice half a world away than by oppression and discrimination half a block from home — *Rowan, Carl* [1925 - 2000; American journalist; author]

Most people have a harder time letting themselves love than finding someone to love — *Russell, Bill* [1934 -; champion basketball athlete]

Ignorance is bold and loud — *Salle, John* [musical artist]

The baobab disappears only on the same spot in which it has lived — *Salle, John*

Our chief usefulness to humanity rests on our combining power with high purpose. Power undirected by high purpose spells calamity, and high purpose by itself is utterly useless if the power to put it into effect is lacking — *Sankara, Thomas* [1949-1987; activist, military leader]

There can be no pity for the slave who refuses to liberate himself – *Sankara, Thomas*

It is appallingly obvious our technology has exceeded our humanity – *Sankara, Thomas*

The world is a stage, but the play is badly cast – *Sankara, Thomas*

I am more dangerous dead – *Saro-Wiwa, Ken.* [1941-1995; Nigerian novelist, environmental activist]

Guinea would be a happier place without Guineans - *Sassine, Williams* [1944 – 1997; Guinean novelist]

African writers are *ecri-vains*; they write in vain, and have no audience – *Sassine, Williams*

We have finished the job, what shall we do with the tools? – *Selasie, Haile* [1891 –1974; Regent / Emperor of Ethiopia, 1916 -1974]

However long it stays in the river the tree trunk cannot become a crocodile – *Sembene, Ousmane* [1923-2007; writer]

Art is animated by invisible forces that rule the universe – *Senghor, L.S.* [1906-2001; poet, philosopher. Co-founder of the *Negritude* movement]

I have made it a habit to be suspicious of the mere music of words – *Senghor, L.S.*

All change, all production and generation are effected through the word – *Senghor, L.S*

I feel, therefore I am – *Senghor, L.S.*

You cannot make yourself whole again by brooding one hundred percent of the time on the darkness of the world – *Sertima, Van Ivan* [1935-2009; international educator on the global Black Experience]

Self-reliance is the fine road to independence – *Shadd, May Ann* [1823-1893; Emancipationist, journalist]

Never leave an enemy behind or it will rise again to fly at your throat – *Shaka* [1787-1828; Zulu king, war leader]

Our desire to be free has got to manifest itself in everything we are and do – *Shakur, Assata* [1947-; African-American activist]

Death is not the greatest loss in life. The greatest loss is the desire that dies inside while still alive – *Shakur, Tupac* [1971-1996; African-American singer-songwriter]

The only thing that comes to a sleeping man is dreams
– *Shakur, Tupac*

I would rather die among yonder gallows than live in slavery – *Sharpe, Samuel* [1801-1832; Abolitionist, Jamaica national hero]

We have defeated Jim Crow, but now we have to deal with his son, James Crow Jr., esquire – *Sharpton, Al* [1954 –; African-American preacher, Civil rights activist]

I always beat the sun up in the morning. It's the secret to why I'm double trouble - *Sharpton, Al*

When you work for something, you appreciate it more – *Smiley, Tavis* [1964-; journalist]

If you are not present during my struggle, don't expect to be present during my success – *Smith, Will* [1968-; African-American actor]

There is no reason to have a Plan B because it distracts from Plan A – *Smith, Will*

If you don't fight for what you want, don't cry for what you lost – *Smith, Will*

Because the media did not create us, the media cannot destroy us – *Sobukwe, Mangaliso* [1924-1978; Emancipationist, founder of the Pan-Africanist Congress (Azania), South Africa]

Nurture is mightier than nature – *Solarin, Tai* [1922-1994; social thinker, author]

Looking at faces of people, one gets the feeling there's a lot of work to be done – *Soyinka, Wole* [1934-; literary author]

We can do for ourselves what nobody else can – *Still, William* [1821-1902; African-American freedom fighter]

No matter the colour of the skin, the blood always remains red – *Talla, André* [1950-; musician]

You can buy a bed but not sleep; You can buy a book but not knowledge – *Tabou Combo* [Haitian music band established in 1968]

Beware the wedge driver; watch his poisonous tongue – *Tambo, Oliver* [1917-1993; South African freedom fighter]

In a sick world, it is the first duty of the artist to get well – *Toomer, Jean* [1894-1967; novelist]

Everybody wants to go to heaven, but nobody wants to die – *Tosh, Peter* [1944-1987; reggae superstar. poet]

To have the truth in your possession you can be found guilty, sentenced to death – *Tosh, Peter*

You ain't gonna miss your water until your well runs dry – *Tosh, Peter*

The power to define is the most important power we have. He is master who can define – *Toure, Kwame* [1941-1998; Pan-Africanist, Civil Rights leader & activist, writer]

We have always tried to be Americans first and Africans all the way down the end. And that is why we are catching hell the way we are catching it today – *Toure, Kwame*

If the enemy is not doing anything against you, you are not doing anything – *Toure, Sekou* [1922-1984; freedom fighter, politician]

The nature and the quality of our connection to the world owe much to our perception of ourselves — *Traore, Aminata* [1947 – ; social & economic rights activist]

I never ran my train off the track, and I never lost a passenger—*Tubman, Harriet* [1822-1913; Emancipationist]

If I could have convinced more slaves that they were slaves, I could have freed thousands more — *Tubman, Harriet*

I had reasoned this out in my mind, there was one of two things I had a right to, liberty or death; if I could not have one, I would have the other — *Tubman, Harriet*

Never wound a snake; kill it — *Tubman, Harriet*

You'll be free or die! — *Tubman, Harriet*

It is the mind that makes the body — *Truth, Sojourner* [1797-1883; Emancipationist]

We do as much, we eat as much, we want as much — *Truth, Sojourner*

I know the difference between black magic and white magic — *Turner, Tina* [1939-; singer-entertainer]

A person is a person because he recognizes others as persons — *Tutu, Desmond* [1931-; priest, humanist, freedom fighter]

Be nice to whites, they need you to rediscover their humanity — *Tutu, Desmond*

I am a leader by default, only because nature does not allow a vacuum – *Tutu, Desmond*

If an elephant has its foot on the tail of a mouse and you say that you are neutral, the mouse will not appreciate your neutrality – *Tutu, Desmond*

To be impartial...is indeed to have taken sides already...with the status quo – *Tutu, Desmond*

My humanity is bound up in yours, for we can only be human together – *Tutu, Desmond*

Those who invest in South Africa should not think they are doing us a favor; they are here for what they get out of our cheap and abundant labor – *Tutu, Desmond*

We may be surprised at the people we find in heaven. God has a soft spot for sinners. His standards are quite low – *Tutu, Desmond*

Without forgiveness, there's no future –*Tutu, Desmond*

Hope is being able to see that there is light despite all of the darkness – *Tutu, Desmond*

There is ability in every disability – *Ukaeze, Obinna* [Nollywood writer/director]

My philosophy is I'm raising future adults, not children – *Usher, Terry Raymond* [1978-; African-American musician]

If you can't be with the one you love, love the one you are with – *Vandross, Luther* [1951-2005; African-American singer]

The surest way to lose a match is to play against the one who invented the rules – *Vianney, Jean-M.* [Afri-Canadian journalist]

Any serious attempt to try to do something worthwhile is ritualistic – *Walcott, Derek* [1930 - 2017; poet]

No person is your friend who demands your silence, or denies your right to grow–*Walker, Alice* [194 -; novelist]

In nature nothing is perfect and everything is perfect – *Walker, Alice*

Childhood has no forebodings; but then, it is soothed by no memories of outlived sorrow – *Walker, Margaret* [1915-1998; novelist, poet]

Character is power – *Washington, Booker T.* [1856-1915; freedom fighter, public intellectual]

Character, not circumstances, makes the man – *Washington, Booker T.*

It is at the bottom of life that we must begin, not at the top – *Washington, Booker T.*

Excellence is to do a common thing in an uncommon way – *Washington, Booker T.*

Few things can help an individual more than to place responsibility on him, and to let him know that you trust him – *Washington, Booker T.*

Success is to be measured not so much by the position that one has reached in life as by the obstacles which he has had to overcome while trying to succeed –*Washington, Booker T.*

I shall allow no man to belittle my soul by making me hate him – *Washington, Booker T.*

If you want to lift yourself up, lift up someone else – *Washington, Booker T.*

No race can prosper till it learns that there is as much dignity in tilling a field as in writing a poem – *Washington, Booker T.*

Nothing ever comes to one, that is worth having, except as a result of hard work *–Washington, Booker T.*

One man cannot hold another man down in the ditch without remaining down in the ditch with him *– Washington, Booker T.*

There are two ways of exerting one's strength: one is pushing down, the other is pulling up *–Washington, Booker T.*

Education is the key to unlock the golden door of freedom *– Washington, Carver. G.* [1860-1943; inventor, farmer]

I love to think of nature as an unlimited broadcasting station, through which God speaks to us every hour, if we will only tune in *– Washington, Carver G.*

If you love it enough, anything will talk with you *– Washington, Carver G*

Learn to do common things uncommonly well *– Washington, Carver G.*

Reading about nature is fine, but if a person walks in the woods and listens carefully, he can learn more than what is in books, for they speak with the voice of God – *Washington, Carver G.*

When you can do the common things of life in an uncommon way, you will command the attention of the world – *Washington, Carver G.*

Where there is no vision, there is no hope – *Washington, Carver G*

Luck is when an opportunity comes along and you're prepared for it – *Washington, Denzel* [1954-; African-American actor]

If I had kept all the money I spent I would have been a millionaire a long time ago – *Waters, Muddy* [1913-1983; African-American blues musician]

You can't lead the people if you don't love the people. You can't save the people if you don't serve the people – *West, Cornel* [1953-; African-American thinker, author]

We need the courage to be impatient with evil and patient with people – *Cornel West*

I am a prisoner of hope – *West, Cornel*

Man is a wrecked vessel – *West, Cornel*

You can't move forward until you look back – *West, Cornel*

To live is to wrestle with despair, yet never allow despair to have the last word – *West, Cornel*

If the best is yet to come the present will blend with it beautifully – *West, Dorothy* [1907-1998; African-American writer]

There is no life that does not contribute to history – *West, Dorothy*

No black history becomes significant and meaningful unless it is taught in the context of the world and national history. In its sealed-off black studies centers, it will be simply another exercise in racial breast-feeding – *Wilkins, Roy* [1901-1981]

You can't do right wrong and you can't do wrong right – *Wilson, Amos* [1941-1995; African-American psychologist]

If we don't know who we are then we are whoever somebody says we are – *Wilson, Amos*

History is an instrument of power – *Wilson, Amos*

Lots of people want to ride with you in the limo, but what you want is someone who will take the bus with you when the limo breaks down – *Winfrey, Oprah* [1954-; African-American broadcaster, media entrepreneur]

Where there is no struggle, there is no strength – *Winfrey, Oprah*

The only people who never tumble are those who never mount the high wire – *Winfrey, Oprah*

When I look into the future, it's so bright it burns my eyes – *Winfrey, Oprah*

Superstition is believing in things you do not understand – *Wonder, Stevie* [1950-;African-American activist, musician]

When you believe in things you don't understand, you suffer – *Wonder, Stevie*

Even schools for Negroes, then, are places where they must be convinced of their inferiority! – *Woodson, Carter G.* [1875- 1950; author, Founder, Black History Week, U.S]]

If a race has no history, if it has no worthwhile tradition, it becomes a negligible factor in the thought of the world, and it stands in danger of being exterminated – *Woodson, Carter G.*

In fact, the confidence of the people is worth more than money – *Woodson, Carter G.*

If the Negro in the ghetto must eternally be fed by the hand that pushes him into the ghetto, he will never become strong enough to get out of the ghetto – *Woodson, Carter G.*

The mere imparting of information is not education – *Woodson, Carter G.*

When you control a man's thinking you do not have to worry about his actions – *Woodson, Carter G.*

Men can starve from a lack of self-realization as much as they can from a lack of bread – *Wright, Richard* [1908-1960; African-American writer]

If a man confesses anything on his death bed, it is the truth; for no man can stare death in the face and lie – *Wright, Richard*

Make up your mind, Snail! You are half inside your house, And halfway out! –*Wright, Richard*

The white folks like for us to be religious, then they can do what they want to with us – *Wright, Richard*

Wealth is a state of mind, and anyone can acquire a wealthy state of mind by thinking rich thoughts – *Young, Andrew* [1932-; Civil Rights activist]

If you're a preacher, you talk for a living, so even if you don't make sense, you learn to make nonsense eloquently – *Young, Andrew*

On the soft bed of luxury many kingdoms have expired – *Young, Andrew*

No one who's white thinks he's innocent. No one who's black thinks he's guilty – *Young, Andrew*

Influence is like a savings account. The less you use it, the more you've got –*Young, Andrew*

We rise in glory as we sink in pride – *Young, Andrew*

It is a blessing to die for a cause, because you can so easily die for nothing – *Young, Andrew*

It is better to be prepared for an opportunity and not have one than to have an opportunity and not be prepared

– *Young, Whitney Moore, Jr.* [1921 – 1971; Civil rights leader and activist]

The hardest work in the world is being out of work – *Young, Whitney Moore, Jr.*

Liberalism seems to be related to the distance people are from the problem –*Young, Whitney Moore, Jr.*

Man has invented weapons of mass destruction but is incapable of a solution against the mosquito – *Zao Zoba, Casimir* [1953-; composer & singer]

Printed in the United States
By Bookmasters